Good Party

ALSO BY JEFF WEDDLE

Dead Man's Hand (Poetic Justice Books, 2019)

A Puncher's Chance (Rust Belt Press, 2019)

Citizen Relent (Unlikely Books, 2019)

It's Colder than Hell / Starving Elves Eat Reindeer Meat / Santa Claus is Dead (Alien Buddha Press, 2018)

Heart of the Broken World (Nixes Mate Books, 2017)

Comes to This (Nixes Mate Books, 2017)

When Giraffes Flew (Southern Yellow Pine, 2015)

The Librarian's Guide to Negotiation: Winning Strategies for the Digital Age (co-author, Information Today 2012)

Betray the Invisible (OEOCO, 2012)

Bohemian New Orleans: The Story of the Outsider and Loujon Press (University Press of Mississippi, 2007)

Good Party

poems by
Jeff Weddle

Poetic Justice Books
Port St. Lucie, Florida

©2020 Jeff Weddle

book design and layout: SpiNDec, Port Saint Lucie, FL
cover image: still image from video *Ros Sothea - Chnam oun Dop-Pram Muy*, ©2018 Kris Haggblom

All rights reserved.

No part of this book may be used or reproduced in any manner whatsoever without written permission except in the case of brief quotations embodied in critical articles and reviews. Members of educational institutions and organizations wishing to photocopy any of the work for classroom use, or authors, artists and publishers who would like to obtain permission for any material in the work, should contact the publisher.

Published by Poetic Justice Books
Port Saint Lucie, Florida
www.poeticjusticebooks.com

ISBN: 978-1-950433-55-1

FIRST EDITION
10 9 8 7 6 5 4 3 2 1

Always for Jill

contents

What I Expect	3
Quite Contrary	4
There Are Many Like That	5
White People Church	7
This Is When, Right Now	9
It Has Happened Again	11
Good Party	12
The Very Second	13
Troubadours	14
The Geography of Caring	15
True Aleph	16
The True Aleph Appears	17
Stop Me If You've Heard This	18
Wild Thing	19
Same with You?	20
The Pretty Hands	21
Things Break	22
Tuscaloosa Twilight	23
No One Gets Out	25
What I Know	26
Human	27
Job Over	28
That's Typical	29
By This We Are Known	30
Something Like This	31
We Shall Tell	33
His Turn and Then	34
Sasha	35

We Could Still Make It	37
Fear This	38
A Bad Night at Home	39
Art	41
It Would Be Nice	42
Underground	43
What I Care About	44
My People	45
Lunch Time	46
Reading the Great Poet	47
The Whole of the Law	49
If You Let It	50
Mystery	51
Don't Wait	52
All of It Gone, But Still	53
Lost Generation	54
How to Write a Poem	55
Mama's Got to Work	56
You Know This	57
To the Guy at the Crosswalk	58
There Is Fire	59
Zephyr	60
Do Not Forget the Small Things	61
Set You Free	62
The Same	63
Still Chained	64
Humanity After	65
The Dream	66
Wolf Tales	67

Bad Weather Coming	69
Don't Be Fooled	71
With All My Might	72
Easy Come, Easy Go	73
Singular Moment	74
Get Ahead! Impress Women! Learn Telepathy Now!	75
A Major New Voice in Contemporary Poetics	76
Forget It	77
Madonna Who Left Too Soon	78
It was decided you are brave	80
And the Feast	81
As Will You	82
Endlessly	83
Another Lonely Night	84
Out of the Trenches	85
Damned Wolves	86
The Beautiful Shoes	87
In America	90
Zappa Zappa Zappa	91
Almost Alchemy	92
Old snapshots from other people's lives	94
Saturday Afternoon	95
These Things When I was Old	96
Look Closely	97
That Day with All the Commotion	98

Good Party

What I Expect

Sometime tomorrow
I expect my daughter
will begin crying at her desk
because she is reading a book
I gave her,

a sad and beautiful book.

And she is taking it to school
where she hopes to finish it,
with no idea
how sad the ending will be.

A book I want her to read now
because some day
the hard ending will truly come
and will arrive
with no book to blame.

And it is good to get a small taste
of that now
laced as this book is with beauty.

But I wish I could be with her
tomorrow
when the book tells her
its cutting truth

and dry her eyes
and hold her close to me

as I have done each day
of her innocence.

As I will do for as long
as she will allow.

Quite Contrary

I
We watched the birds as long as we could stand it
and the morning was silent like inside a cloud.
Mary had her blade back inside her boot
and my pistol felt like a rock
tucked into the waist of my pants.
The people in the house had children
and that was always bad.
When it was time we gathered ourselves
and started down the hill,
Mary staring straight ahead
and the birdsong suddenly everywhere.

II
Mary at the window and Mary by the door
and Mary in the darkness and Mary on the floor
and Mary tells the kids goodnight
and Mary with her charms
and Mary with her little knife
doing everybody harm.

III
We forget how it ends, but it does end.
Finally. Mary without her knife.
Me without my gun.
Perhaps we are in boxes somewhere cold.
Perhaps something else.
Mary used to sing little songs of praise.
I remember they were beautiful.

IV
The birds watched until we became tiresome.
When they flew away, each vowed to return
at an agreed upon time. How I wonder if they ever did.

There Are Many Like That

there must be
many people
who are not dead
and tarted up
like dried flowers

many who are not
pretending

there must be many
who have not been
shredded, folded
and tucked into
dark places
where breathing
is the best
they can hope for

many who have not
gone missing
in the screams
of the day

many who thrive
in the dense
inescapable
clockwork

I surely pass them on the streets
or speak with them in the grocery
or watch them on my television

they must be
everywhere
with secrets
I can only guess

these happy
these chosen

as I sit on my couch
with my old cat

everything quiet

the two of us
waiting for the
cheap blessings
of nightfall

and though I cannot
speak for the cat

I am like the remainder
of the world

tarted up
folded

and falling headfirst
into darkness

White People Church

Small men
with dense books
they think
they understand

angry women
on their knees

thumping thumping

hate called love
love called sin
death called glory

children taught
to bind themselves
to this

small men
angry women

thumping thumping

children dressed
in pretty clothing
bored and afraid

boys and girls
wishing they were
anywhere else

glancing sideways
at each other

and looking
to be
saved

This Is When, Right Now

When words carried
the wind away
and fire cleansed our hands

when words drowned
the snakes in the garden
and soaked up the blood
and soaked up the young girl's tears

when words bit
through the dark
until the dark screamed

when words stopped dancing
and got real mean

when Octavio Paz
spoke of his city

and Bukowski
spoke of his city

and Sandburg
spoke of his city

and Hemingway spoke of Paris

when words knew they meant nothing
and everything depended upon them

when night got so cold
our teeth chattered

when the sun died out

when all of us were ready for anything
and nothing is
what happened

It Has Happened Again

The commonplace horror
of bullets released
into crowds of strangers
of babies shot
and mothers
giving themselves
as shields
or begging God
to go back one day.

The banal terror
of anger on fire
or bored losers
with a few hundred rounds
and an afternoon to kill.

What will you do about it?

It has come for you
even if the blood
is not yet on your body.
It is already on your hands.

Good Party

Drunk in someone's kitchen
and the most beautiful girl
in the world
wandered in
and I told her so
as I kissed her
right there
in front of her boyfriend
and she was happy
and I was happy
and he laughed
and I had another beer
and they wandered off
and I never
saw either of them
again

The Very Second

I did not dream of you
my dreams are not so welcome
I did not find your spirit in my pocket
I saw you turn the corner
that was it
the sun was almost up
and it was cold
someone said something
I didn't quite get
as you came into view
my dreams were nowhere
in the electric dawn
as everything became your face

Troubadours

A nod to
barstool saints

tattered promise

reckless hearts
forgiving of sin

Hank died
and people wept

Blaze died
and the air
went out
of the world

Townes died
and a door swung shut

A nod to blessings
from dark places

The song
never shared
is the loveliest dream

The Geography of Caring

In the attic eating skin
in the dog's belly
in the baby's rotten leg
in the ill mind
in the storm a'brewing
in the crawl space with the rats
in the delicate pattern
in the food with the lid replaced
in the blood shocked hands
in the practiced smile
in the forced tears
in the bright sunlight
in the fever dream
in the acid
in the hidden bones
in the attic eating flesh
in the abandoned automobile
in the dark freezer
in the set trap
in the unsuspected kiss
in the shadows of your room
in the shallow grave
in the unopened letter
in the festering wound
in the compromise with grace
in the attic with what remains
knowing where you are
knowing where you are
knowing where you are

True Aleph

The true aleph
if it is anything at all
must be a poem
not yet written

a potential poem
of clarity and flow

nothing complex

the true aleph
so hard to reach

this true aleph
buried inside
the timeless mind

beware the aleph
that appears

for it is a false aleph
bounded by
its moment

beware the prophets
who say
it has been revealed

the true aleph
is hidden
if it is anything at all

guard it with me
it is inside
you now

The True Aleph Appears

When the true aleph appeared
it was first ignored
then mocked then reviled

the people said
there could be no aleph
and besides this wasn't it

everyone knew this
except newborns and the dying
who saw it true
and only for a flash

because the true aleph
cannot appear
in this bounded world

as everyone knows
as you have been told

Stop Me If You've Heard This

An aleph walks into a bar
says to the bartender
gimme a drink
bartender says
got any ID?
the aleph says
nothing
for it is the
void

Wild Thing

That time into the wild
you said something I am sure
we all misheard
something like
a leak or a combustion
a curious
circus of noise

The wild is perfect for that
if you don't fret danger
and I suppose you don't

Later the wild was a laugh fest
with the consumption of the flesh
the drinking of the blood
the wearing of the taken items
but things were jangly for a while

That time into the wild
you said a love sonnet
in a brand new language
spoke it
right out loud

Where are you now?
Everyone wonders
if you still love us
or if you killed our final chances
but no one does
a damned thing to find out

Same with You?

One opens the door
with expectations of relief
or the purring of cats

one opens the door
with memories of cold wind

one opens the obscure door
with insistent curiosity

one opens the door
with a cracked mind
forgetting how dogs often howl

one sometimes gets dizzy

one sometimes opens the door
and never thinks to close it

one disregards the door
and dreams

The Pretty Hands

And then folded, put away,
left in the heavy dark
like a gift
of unfashionable linen
from a maiden aunt
years ago
forgotten in a drawer
while the pretty hands
that did this
finally wither
and no one remembers
either the linen
or you
and no one lasts the night

Things Break

There will be things to learn
like the proper temperature
to cook eggs (low and slow is best
even if fast and hot is easier
and quicker to the plate)

and how to avoid
carelessly breaking
the yolk

or the heart of another

and, yes, how to protect your own.

This is more complicated
than cooking eggs
and, in truth, maybe impossible
if you want also to have
a splendid life.

Poorly cooked eggs
and broken hearts
happen
in the yawning of
the day-to-day.

No one wants to go slow
and most wind up with
good enough eggs
and unsettled hearts.

Enjoy.

TUSCALOOSA TWILIGHT
for Danny Vera

One hundred miles from Tuscaloosa
Heading up to Kentucky

I've got this road and got my memories
I don't need no company

Left her standing in the twilight
In the coming of the rain

In the Tuscaloosa twilight
I won't see that girl again

One hundred miles from Tuscaloosa
this road will take me where it will

Maybe there I'll meet another
in the cold Kentucky hills
In the cold Kentucky hills

One hundred miles from Tuscaloosa
The rain is pouring down on me

All the reasons for my sorrows
Are the things that set me free

That girl was kind and she was pretty
Just the type to settle down

In the Tuscaloosa twilight
I left her standing in that town

One hundred miles from Tuscaloosa
Kentucky calling out my name

The cold hills of east Kentucky
And the easing of my pain
And the easing of my pain

No One Gets Out

You walk like there is
an empty space
beside you
alone in bright hallways
where a secret, unsent letter
is welcome company

but chestnut hair damp
across crumpled sheets
describes the sweetest dream.

The crazy man on the corner
said music
inside the instrument
not yet conceived
would kill for freedom
and I suppose that's right.

I wonder if you know
shadows bleed
uncanny lyrics
to explain riddles
posed in unknown lands.

I wonder if you know
you move like a song.

What I Know

I'm easily confused
but some things are clear:

when you tire of being bald
you wear a hat

when your eyes weaken
you wear glasses

when you are alone
you find a dog

I'm easily confused
but some things I know:

when the world weeps, weep
become the clown as needed

allow yourself to be the darkness
and also the rose

I'm easily confused but I know
how to wear a hat and glasses

somewhere I have a dog
and I want to be the rose

Human

In the final cradle, no heartbeat
in the withering sun
in the lateness of the hour
in the sad faces
in the crowded streets
in the old car that has quit at the worst time
in the memory of hope
in the last chance and the tries after
in the empty blessings
in the broken silence
in the worn gingham at the final dance
in the cold flesh
in the still moment
in the invitation never sent
in the disregarded touch
in the final cradle
in the beginning
in the end
in the unopened letter
in the necessary goodbyes
all of it
all of it over

Job Over

When the world ended
they cut away all flesh
and found at last
the angels all hidden
in gutters
in the hearts of dogs
in half empty bottles
of sour mash
and they gathered
the angels
for disposal
in the usual way
and when it was done
they were satisfied
set the cleansing blaze
and moved on

That's Typical

I
Following myself along the sidewalk
and taking pains to step on my shadow.
One of us stumbles.

II
Oh, the conversations one has
when one is lucid and alone.

III
Following down the dark hills
to far, far away
where the shadow has no purchase.

IV
What has been hidden
becomes slapstick
in the inky vast chitchat.

V
You take the dice and roll.
No choice.
Everyone believes you.
Everyone is understood to cheer.

By This We Are Known

the vast space
between here
and dreams
in the study
of starlight

the child wishes
to be also ancient
or outside time

someone should tell him
the saving lie

that stars are their own stories
not his to know

but why would he
ever listen?

Something Like This

days like dreams
where small creatures
maintain balance
with the demands of the sky
and impossible fish
swim the romance
of deep currents

highways to new towns
where unknown loves wait
in small apartments
littered with cheap mementos
you will come
to cherish

an old waitress serving
hot coffee and cherry pie
in an ancient diner
hanging on by hope

days like brass concerts
on the city green
hotdogs and smiles all around

wise children holding hands
with the dying

days of tears
because tears
are often needed

everyone who ever was
stitched into the quilt
of what will someday be

the world still possible
and all of it breathing

and you with your brilliant flesh
alive in the dance
for one more minute

We Shall Tell

stones and water
wind come large

earth needful
obliging fire

wind and water
stones

pages battered
and gone

this is what
we shall tell

at the end
these stories

His Turn and Then

When death came to his bull heart
and the mind it governed

When his sinews when his blood
when his flesh ceased

When time became no time

When death came to his bull heart
and the flower of his dreaming

explosions of light consumed
all blood flesh sinew
consumed his bull heart

When death became the flower of his dreaming
faded to blunt silence

When the words he had written
were all that remained

When death came to his bull heart
no one knew him and still some wept

When the days were left for those
in the embrace of faltered illusion
and everyone walked away

night was still night and morning came
as it always would and there were still
some who dreamed

their bull hearts beating against
what would break in them too soon

Sasha

My cat believes herself
to be dazzling
and I allow her
the fantasy
for old times' sake
as she comes
to the kitchen table
where I sit
attempting tasks
less important
than stroking
her head

She flashes her tail
in the heavy air
and claws my hand

the old coquette
demanding love

and says something
that sounds quite
cosmopolitan
though I have never
fully mastered
the nuances of
her kind's tongue

My cat finds herself
finished with me
and glides away
without looking back

whatever I was trying to do
forgotten and shown up
for its hollow vanity

the two of us aware
of who is in control
and reminded
that she still has
her moments
of dazzle

We Could Still Make It

If we could go back
to Yasgur's farm
and find the garden
that never was
if we could be golden
for a second
if the bullets
could be rendered
unspent
if we could be the music
we always meant
ourselves to be

Fear This

If you must fear
then fear the poet

fear the one
who brings light
to the secret places
of your tender heart

the places which
before that moment
you never saw

this is the beauty
that will kill you
sure as a blade
or love
or a last glance
in darkness

it will kill you like that
brutal and true

every time
foolhardy

you allow

A Bad Night at Home

The rain came hard and water
got in beneath the doors.

Soon there was
an inch or more in the hall.

Somehow the child got outside.
The hog, too.

We ran into the night
and there were people
everywhere
with their signs,
angry and chanting.

Marjorie went for the hog.
I chased the child.

Neither of us had any luck.

The rain kept coming.

The people kept chanting
and waving signs
in their angry way.

We never saw the child
or the hog again.

Our floors were ruined.

Next time we would know better
than to let a hog or a child
roam free,
even in the living room.

Next time would be different.

Art

It's too much
and everything
has been said

all the others said it

too much clutter
confused frequencies

the world is a ball
on a tether
orbiting to its
final stop

nothing left
to hit

It's too much
and every
small thing
weighs tons

all the others
already told you

greedy bastards

nothing left
to say

It Would Be Nice

It would be nice to write
a love poem
or about the beautiful things
that live in forests

it would be nice to write about days
when everything fits
when the gears of life
are not broken in the teeth

when sorrow is not the hole
in the center of the world

it would be nice
to write about road trips with friends
adventures into mystery
that end with great stories
and laughter

it would be nice to live in a world
where children in cages
were not a commonplace
where America did not
act out its Nazi wet dreams

it would be nice if there were a way
to go home

Underground

stolen notes
playing
in dark corners

damp air
fragrant
with promise

beneath a dream
of skin

watching her
walk like
music

into a small house
shuttered
against touch
and its lessons

the scripture
of melodic
night

What I Care About

Life on Mars
and blue
mason jars
sweet tea
and flowers
and you

My People

Some grow up shy
and in constant love
with the world

and always with the one
who is out of reach
or seems to be

some grow up watching clouds
and crying over butterflies

the light they seek
is necessary
but never enough

too much happens
in the world

some find their way through it
some never do

all of these
are my dear ones

all of them

and I mean you
most of all

Lunch Time

That's what the ruby trees are for
all glittering in the waves

that's the reason for swans
as if swans needed a reason

that's why we keep our secret letters
like the one you wrote

about that barbecue stand on the corner
near our window

and how you wanted to be everyone's forever
not just yours and mine

though you were quite hungry
and the details could wait

while the ruby trees danced in water
and held to empty delight

and the swans bent their necks in prayer
and I went out for sweet tea, pulled pork and slaw

with the sidewalk singing beneath my feet
and every crumb of time smiling your name

Reading the Great Poet

I read the great poet
and wrote
a single poem
from the inspiration
of his words

a poem that pleased me
for a moment

and I have it somewhere
most likely in my notes
but I doubt
I would recognize it now
if it fell into my hands

just a jumble of words

as the great poet
lies in a grave
in some foreign land

and people read his work
and weep
and no one knows
my name

as I pull a book
by the great poet
from my shelf

and try to feel something
that might tell me
what to do

then close it
having found nothing

wondering what I thought
I was doing
in the first place

The Whole of the Law

do great things
in the shadow
of time
as you will
oh, Babylon
oh, Babylon

do these outside
the great shadow
of your will
in the timeless time
oh, Babylon
oh, Babylon

do as you will
in the darkness and light
do as you will
in the hard embrace
oh, Babylon
oh, Babylon

If You Let It

Down in the basement
where bad decisions
sway their braggy
smoke-stained colors
down the dark staircase
down the lost corridors
where unremembered
dreams sink lower
down in the private dark
the liquid silence
even there the visions
even there sometimes beauty
the terrible heart will have its way

Mystery

What the cat sees
in the fractured air
may live or not
but it surely dances

Don't Wait

Everything crumbles
everything good courts death
the walls will someday fail
ceilings will buckle
all inspiration will drown in rain
everything will choke on mud
night is coming
and no shelter can brace you
children last for a minute
and are lost on the wind

All of It Gone, But Still

Hints of lost a poet
in the veins
of oak leaves
scattered through years

in the ash of a single
burned page

in wind on bare hands

hints of once
commonplace magic
now forgotten

hints of royal bloodline
in beggar child fingers

hints of abundance
hints of heroic sacrifice

hints of waves
on a rocky coast
now gone for ages

hints of a lost poem
a true painting of the true god

hints of our connection

our blood
our hearts
our futile, necessary courage

Lost Generation

To live in Paris
call it 1920s
back streets
and street lamps
bricks underfoot
and her waiting
in the starry night rain
liquid in that thin
blue cotton dress
the one that kills you
she ready to break
your heart
and you desperate
for her to do it
who wouldn't want
such a death?

How to Write a Poem

Open up and let it breathe
listen to the lines as they come
and get them down
as close as you can
wear it like a shawl
and cast it off
when you are ready
give it to anybody
who is willing
give thanks
move on

Mama's Got to Work

Mama's got to go now, children,
Mama's got to go.

The streets are filled with silver, children,
and Mama's got to go.

The men will buy us bread and milk
and maybe a little wine.

Mama's got to go now, children,
and bring home something fine.

Mama's got to go to work
and won't come back alone.

Mama loves you very much.

Don't make a sound
when I bring him home.

You Know This

The one you seek
is the lost book
longed for in the dark
the undiscovered island
the moon that once was
the chord that fingers
cannot play
the dance of words
sacred to mystery
imagined
but out of reach

To the Guy at the Crosswalk

I'm sorry, dude
I would have stopped
if you had been
a pretty girl
but you weren't
so that's
on you.

There Is Fire

Each secret is ancient
and fills us like smoke.

Finally we walk with others
dressed in black clothing
and most things become stone.

Each lie has been told forever
sometimes to trusting eyes
sometimes to eyes more knowing.

Do not think yourself clever.

This is only the music
which puts each of us
to our tasks
and you play it just passing fair.

Each secret is the beauty
we allow to wither alone

as we become smoke
and vanish
like silly promises
of love and always
in the vast and hungry
empty
burning night.

Zephyr

It's like a photograph
of a little boy, circa 1963:
striped shirt, crew cut.
He's wrapped around his father
as the father reads the funny pages.
Tiny fingers drape that big neck,
caught forever in vivid
black and white:
You can feel the smiles.
You can read the laughter.

Do Not Forget the Small Things

Lacey tablecloths and sheer curtains
or wind bending green branches
in bright April

the perfect angle of sunlight
on an important, particular day

when children
cried and laughed
all at once
and old age
accepted its season
with joy

do not forget the infinity
of after and before
the blessings of melody
the gift of touch

the one you loved who never knew it
or the ones who always did

do not forget you are here
in the smallest things
and memories of best days

do not forget my arms around you
the secrets we managed to keep
or the stars we loved so well

Set You Free

Christ
Mohammed
God

The stories
We are told

Rich man's locks
Poor man's prison

The Same

in the end
you can't know

death is only
for the dying

but life has just
two possibilities:

it means
everything

or it means
nothing

by miracle chance
these are the same

Still Chained

free mind of now
of the moment

this one
free romp
through quark
and cosmos

free mind
goddess mind
genuine article mind

faith be damned

free mind
on a cold Sunday
in December

mind like a monkey
scampering mind
mind throwing poop

lost mind
free free free

so long mind
be well

Humanity After

suddenly friends
in that confusion
the noise of attack
of shattered glass
smashed stone
taken in as best
as possible
bleeding grief
wanting shared coffee
to mean what it
once meant
praying over
the deaths
of strangers
friends now
finding a road out
finding a way
then parting
the world
locked down
no place
for music
anywhere

The Dream

This voice, America
boisterous and loud
this song, this open sky
this long highway
this voice, America
these wheels and wings
these musical people
this light
this voice
these sounds of confusion
wanting to heal
the work of America
this voice this nation
these people that we are
we the people
the air about us
this swagger
hand in hand in hand

Wolf Tales

When the wolf cries boy
and children punish us
for our accidental sins
when our sins
against the children
burn through the bone
when the rain forgives nothing
when the door swings wide
and no one bothers
to enter
when cats
ignore boxes
and old men
lose their minds
but find their hearts
when the wolf cries uncle
when the wolf cries
just cries
when the flowers bloom
out of season
when the children
grow weary
when they grow old
when they wither
when the home team
wins big on the road
and their plane
goes down in flames
when everything matters
and it becomes impossible

to say why
when the girl waits
at the airport
until someone comes for her
drags her away
when the
screaming starts
when the screaming
becomes fierce
when it cannot end
when it can never end

Bad Weather Coming

Almost midnight
and the cat insistent
with her claws
and cold rain
soaking streets
across unrecognizable America
so many sleeping
almost midnight
and the cat gives in
to sleep
and the people
in unrecognizable America
think they have it pretty good
as the cat
sleeps beside me
dreaming her tiger dreams
while my dreams
are swallowed whole
and unrecognizable
in dead America
almost midnight
and faces
I never thought would go
sink into masks of apathy
or masks of hate
masks of stupidity
almost midnight
and I close my eyes
as the cat stirs
settles

and goes back to sleep
in unrecognizable America
where the people
are happy as hell
as the killing
is mostly for sport
and much more
is still to come

Don't Be Fooled

the last fade
is not cold
just a hard burn
inside the skull
a crazy song
wrapped around
the heart
with thorny vines
not cruel
but uncaring
and the sunny smile
you sometimes see
is only the
displaced rot
of the thing
we became
long ago

With All My Might

I hold to what holds me
my children, who will
someday leave
my wife, who is often sad
my dog and cat, who are
doddering old ladies
my parents in their twilight
thinking too much of God
I hold to what holds me
a red teddy bear
missing one eye
a small blanket
with most of the pink
washed out
photographs taken
on meaningless days
for no reason at all
and a few dreams
we meant to try
before we slipped away

Easy Come, Easy Go

Under my skin the thing I found
relatable in the garden
under my nose the thing I found
all furry and small
the thing hissing under my skin
like steam pipes in my father's old apartment
crawling and digging with its tiny fingers
relatable to most according
to demographic breakdown
the statistics don't lie under my skin
the love waits hungry where my fingers
can't reach this thing in my garden
relatable to the few who stuck around
after the tragic separation
when the skin retreated and the thing
I found in my garden went back
to its own affairs and I did my best
to remember the hissing sounds
like steam pipes the time
I was in an old building
for reasons I cannot share

Singular Moment

there is still
something left
not much
but something

still sunlight on grass
still a soft breeze
still the laughter
of children

there is still a chance

there is still
something left

as you stand
beside an open window
as you breathe slowly

knowing they will come for you
certain they will come

they will never have this moment
never take what you have right now

this is all you can keep
but it is enough

sunlight on grass
a soft breeze

memories of
children laughing

Get Ahead! Impress Women! Learn Telepathy Now!

Don't resist. It doesn't matter.
The guy down the street did it
and look at him now.

Good job, pretty wife,
even if she's too thin
and has a faint mustache.

She doesn't scream.

His mind is everywhere. Everyone knows.

His mind hurts when it comes inside the room.
Everyone feels the same.

The guy down the street also has a dog. It's a good dog, probably.
No biting, yet. It may have mange, but no dog is perfect.

No dog can take the course because the course is just for people.
So, there.

The course comes in the mail. Two dollars. Pretty good price.

Don't resist. It doesn't matter.

The mind flows in. The mind flows out.

Everyone tied down. Everyone quiet.

The guy down the street is pure mind now.
He is everywhere. He doesn't scream.

Check every room. If they are not screaming, who is?
Not the child. Not the baby. Something says it is me.

The course works. Best two-dollar investment ever.

A Major New Voice in Contemporary Poetics

Important uttering on trusty keyboard
with chamomile tea and track lighting
cozy sweater and expensive comfy pants

the words practically roll off the fingers
each a pearl a window to the crystal vision.

The framed credentials tucked away.

Getting the pain down
the anger, the injustice.

Such fine words to show the group
to shape it into something else,
maybe something
for the *Georgia Review* or *Poetry*.

All those people sleeping on the streets
and the hungry kids and rape and everything.

And now sipping the tea and now sipping the tea.

Ah, inspiration! A metaphor involving birds!
Birds are always a sure bet—
maybe birds and opioids.

That's popular now in the right circles.

Ploughshares might like this one
and tenure review is right around the corner.

Time to hit the gym,
take the scenic route,
and grab a croissant at Starbucks;

miss all the bums downtown.

Forget It

It is easy to despair when you read them,

each one so concerned, so sincere
so edgy, so with it, so woke, so cosmopolitan,
so coiffed, so ragged in just the proper way.

Even the old ones call to mind words like "precocious."
(Or is precious better? Never mind.
We'll work that out in committee.)

Polished to reflective shine,
hard to see past,

they make me want to be unkind.

Okay, they make me unkind. (Or is queasy better?
Note to committee: we'll need a vote.)

One must remember to hate oneself
if not on the approved list,
though one must still be coiffed, ragged, woke, etc.

There are careers at stake, and everyone knows
how x crushed y and z sat in on n's defense,
and you know how that turned out.

Despair is easy, but reading them is less so.
(The committee understands that
they are the only legitimate readers.)

Open the books:

Nothing there, nothing there, but empty air—
Despair.

Madonna Who Left Too Soon (For Lyn Lifshin)

I imagine her
in jade and silver
or turquoise
perhaps ready
to dance
or perhaps
she was the quiet girl
who didn't mind
being a wallflower
bookish certainly
and so thin
with that long dark hair
in the author photos
where she looked
right at you,
personally,
the frank gaze
of a woman who
has given up all
her secrets
and demands only
your brief attention
as payment

I imagine her
walking along a chilly
nighttime sidewalk
the collar of her jacket
turned up against
a stiff breeze

trying to change
her direction
with only bum luck
for its trouble

I imagine her
pounding the keys
sending fat envelopes
to all the magazines

I imagine her burning
I imagine her fire
I imagine all the poets quiet
for just a moment
and blowing kisses

before we pull
ourselves together
and move on
without her

It was decided you are brave

this is how love finds you
doing nothing by half
deciding you are art
in torn gingham

It was decided you are electric
never going on that holiday to Spain
but always prepared
behind dangerous shades

This is how love finds you
brave by half again

It was decided
you come back for more
cut to pieces
electric

This is how you finish
punk as hell
blistered in glory

Found by love
in torn gingham

And the Feast

In the fearsome night
in the hungry woods
the wicked wolves
go feeding

the wicked wolves
and witches
the starving eyes
go feeding

the witches
and the fledgling child
the spirits all
go feeding

the wicked wolves
the starving child
the killing eyes
go feeding

As Will You

The dead understand
frost and falling
ice
bone silent entry to
falling brilliant
empty the entirety of a single
fading note gone in thunder

Endlessly

A rose tattoo
and the promise
of betrayal

but there are
clean sheets
and that counts
for something

a rose tattoo
above the heart
coffee at noon
and a warm bath

hands that know
the alchemy of skin
and the promise
of nothing
but clean sheets
and nothing
to forget

but the promise
of a rose tattoo
endlessly red
above the heart
a warm bath
and nothing more

this alchemy
of touch
and betrayal

Another Lonely Night

Small crimes
and no one left
so the red haired girl
talks dirty
to the odd boy
in his slouch hat

Broadway dreams
keep her going
and a few dollars
in the sock drawer
means hope
for a bottle
and a laugh
while he keeps
an eye out
for new romance

and the stars above
do what they can
while an unknown person
of questionable means
saunters in so sweetly
to feed on chance and blood
so handsome
and looking for a way
to kill us all

Out of the Trenches

the battle paused
electric in silence
and guns left behind
in that moment
found their best use
as weight
upon the ground
and the soldiers
from one side
and the other
embraced and played
and told stories
of their lives
until somewhere
a mortar fired
signaling retreat
and the time
for killing
came again

Damned Wolves

All of a sudden you became surreal
like a dance of eels on a winter prairie
with wolves starving
somewhere in the distance of fading light.

The wolves did not understand
that you, previously, were not
in any way surreal,
but that didn't change the fact
that they were hungry.

All of a sudden your surreality
became a snowstorm
and the wolves competed
with one another
to catch the most of you
on their tongues
as night overtook the prairie

and you crossed your legs
and sat smoking your cigarette
in our cozy apartment
on the corner of Lost and Silent

in some city that anyone
would recognize
if I were willing to say its name.

All of a sudden I knew I was in love
but the wolves would not let me tell you.

The wolves would not let me say a word.

The Beautiful Shoes

When the boy was twelve
his mother bought him
a pair of shoes
made by the infamous anarchist
Nicola Sacco

although at that time
Sacco was only a not-infamous cobbler
and the shoes were beautiful
and of high quality.

He kept them shined
and wore them to school
on special days
and church on Sundays.

Eventually his feet
got too big to fit into the shoes,
but they were so nice
that he kept them put away
in the back of a closet
just off the kitchen.

Every so often
he took the shoes out
and ran his fingers
over the leather
and remembered things
he had done
while wearing them.

Once, he had been in love
with a beautiful girl
who had been born in Italy
but came to America as a child.

The boy was very shy,
but his beautiful shoes
gave him the courage
to talk to her.

Sadly, nothing came of it
and a few years later
she married a butcher
and died soon after,
in childbirth.

He was grown
the day Sacco
was executed
for a murder
he may or may not
have committed

but the young man
didn't keep up
with current affairs.

And anyway, he didn't know
it was Sacco who had made
his beautiful shoes.

He never forgot
the lovely Italian girl, though.

Her name was Andrea
and he often visited her grave,
imagining how life might have been.

On the day of Sacco's execution,
he was at Andrea's grave.

He imagined himself
young and handsome
in his beautiful shoes.
He imagined himself
with Andrea, dancing,
the shoes upon his feet
and everything floating
in air.

In America

In America where
the best minds stumble
and my friends have died
where the bleeding streets
are ready for explosion
where the starry dynamo of night still hums
where we hate one another
because half of us are crazy
and the rest can't take it anymore

In America where the roads
are choked with rage
where the roads are choked
with shoot 'em up crybaby bigots
where we watch football games
and care about the winners
but not about the hungry family next door
or the homeless with nothing but the street
or the brown skinned people murdered by police
every damned day

In America where we are numb
where we are caught by screens
where night is coming
where fire awaits
where screams will be heard
where screams will echo
where the people will wonder how this happened
in America where all the answers were given
and no one bothered to learn

Zappa Zappa Zappa

Begin Transmission

It is well known that time is fire
that fire consumes
that consuming transforms
that transformation
is the first principle of life
It is well known that life is suffering
that suffering educates
that education is necessary
that necessity
is the mother of invention
It is well known that the Mothers of Invention
backed up Frank Zappa
that Frank Zappa set brains on fire
that fiery brains take time
that consuming Frank Zappa
is education

End Transmission

Almost Alchemy

You find the stone
but assume
it is a turtle
and believing
yourself
earthbound
fail to see
its wings.

You discover
a new species
of light
as brilliant
as your
shadow

and drink
from the stone
thinking it is
only water

or dance
with the wind
as the stone
swallows you.

All these come
like a wound
as the stone
often says.

All these
find you
supplicant
and oblivious,
the stone
left unrecognized

as necessary
as air

fugitive
and unforgiving.

Old snapshots
from other people's lives

The photograph of you
in blue pants
and a lumpy yellow sweater
the one where you
were drinking something
through a straw
on a bright sidewalk
of a forgotten street
the one taken by accident
because you were passing
a statue of someone
who had once been famous
the photograph I never saw
but am sure must exist
somewhere in someone's
photograph album
because there can't be a world
without some small extra part of you
hidden and waiting
like a distant, dancing star
for the shock of discovery
and an ancient, shaking voice
saying so very slowly
"Oh my God. It's you."

Saturday Afternoon

At the bakery, bread
an option of roses

At the gate, an oath
questions of the heart

Watching your careful steps
but look at the time

No time for roses
we are all late to the party

These Things When I was Old

Once, when I was old,
I was born into the body of a calf
and taken to slaughter
where my pieces
were lost on the wind.

Once, when I was old,
I became a butterfly
and flew into the clouds.

Once, when I was old,
I remembered dancing
and I cried.

Once, when I was old,
I saw your face in my own
and destroyed the world
with the depths
of my regret.

Once, when I was old,
I was never seen again.

Look Closely

consider the possibility
this child is the entire point

see her lazing on the couch on a hot day
or contemplating a thunderstorm just as it begins

just as the trees start their dance
and lightning comes crashing

consider the possibility
she is the entire point of the world

that each dust mote is aware of her
that every flower is her servant

that the birds know her name
a name you will never understand

though it be sung so clearly
and carried like music through the air

That Day with All the Commotion

He watched from his window
and saw the world burning

flames shot from the earth
and the heavens

children and animals ran
panicked and aflame

charred mothers cradled balls of fire
that had been babies

from his window he saw armies marching
and heard screams and explosions

men raped women children
babies animals and other men

as people tore each other apart
and ate the bleeding flesh

as scores of airplanes dropped bombs
and grim soldiers with beautiful parachutes

and some of those planes crashed
exploding into the raging crowds

while in the distance
lovely music played

a rousing march
that became louder and louder

as he stared through his window
until finally all was finished

and he examined his fingernails
opened another beer

and wondered what he might do
with the rest of his day

Grateful acknowledgment is made to the following, where some of the poems previously appeared, sometimes in slightly different form:

Alien Buddha Press, Alien Buddha Zine, Gypsy Art Show, Masks are Never Enough, Poetry Feast, Pressure Press Presents, Rust Belt Press, Rust Belt Review, Rogue Wolf Press, The Wingnut Brigade.

Jeff Weddle grew up in Prestonsburg, a small town in the hill country of eastern Kentucky. He has worked as a public library director, disc jockey, newspaper reporter, Tae Kwon Do teacher, and fry cook, among other things. His first book, *Bohemian New Orleans: The Story of the Outsider and Loujon Press* (University Press of Mississippi, 2007), won the Eudora Welty Prize and helped inspire Wayne Ewing's documentary, *The Outsiders of New Orleans: Loujon Press* (Wayne Ewing Films, 2007). He teaches in the School of Library and Information Studies at the University of Alabama.

www.ingramcontent.com/pod-product-compliance
Lightning Source LLC
Chambersburg PA
CBHW030157100526
44592CB00009B/315